New Beginnings

New Beginnings

A Story of Love,
Sacrifice and Growth

Lena Cottingham

ISBN: 978-0-578-42417-0

Copyright © 2019 by Lena Cottingham

No part of this book may be reproduced or transmitted in any form or by any means, graphic, electronic, digital or mechanical, including photocopying, recording, taping, or by any information storage retrieval system, without the permission in writing from the author.

DEDICATION

Coming from a person who never previously picked up a book for fun, suddenly I had a story to write. I want this story to help someone in an abusive relationship who may feel they have nowhere to go. I want this book to equip you with the mindset that material things have no real value when you're living in hell. I want you to keep moving forward, even when you feel the world is against you. I want you to understand life will still continue, even if you feel it's over. Don't ever give up on yourself and your dreams. When you least expect it, the person you thought you lost in your life may walk right back in (YOU). Showing compassion and understanding goes a long way rather than blaming someone for their issues.

I only hope when you finish reading this book you find your INNER STRENGTH, HAPPINESS, INNER PEACE, and direction in your life!

CHAPTER 1

If only she could have foreseen the future of that evening, she would have left sooner.

It was about 10:30 P.M. Laughter and joy filled the home. Everyone was up later than usual. The two children, Anthony and Tasha, were ready for bed, but first they wanted to hear a wise old tale from Jane, their mother. While Jane was telling them a bedtime story, she heard her husband, Marcus, stumbling and shouting out loud coming up the walkway. Jane quickly told the children to go to their room and shut the door. Marcus came into the house in a rage.

Jane nervously asked Marcus, "Honey are you okay? Do you want anything to eat?"

Marcus looked at Jane and he clutched his wife as he had done time and time before.

"What are you doing?" screamed Jane.

Marcus started hitting her and threw her on the floor. Anthony and Tasha sat on their bedroom floor by the door holding each other, pleading as their father continued his rage on their mother. After about ten long minutes of this violent outrage while his wife Jane was pleading for her life, he slowly stopped, then looked deep into her eyes, turned slowly and went quietly to bed. As the atmosphere became quiet, Anthony opened the door and both children ran over to their mother. Jane was slumped down on the kitchen floor against the wall and she held them so tight that they could hardly breathe.

She silently prayed as she was crying and said, "NO MORE... NO MORE!" while shaking her head. She quietly stood up, walked the children to their room and hastily got them both dressed. Since Marcus fell asleep within ten minutes of going to the bedroom, Jane grabbed her purse, shoes, and all three of them silently made a run for it. They left the house with only the clothes they were wearing as her husband was now in a drunken sleep.

CHAPTER 2

When you realize you have nowhere to go but up.

Around 11 P.M., Jane stopped by her favorite cousin's house, Karen, and knocked on the door in a panic. Of course, the entire house awoke and her cousin Karen could not believe what she saw as her husband, Allen, opened the door. Jane had a black eye and was bleeding. Tasha and Anthony stood there crying in fear as they held their mother tight. Jane had made up her mind that she could not take it anymore and that she was leaving town immediately to catch the next bus to Tennessee.

"I need a 'New Beginning' in my life and for my children."

Karen asked, "Where are you going?" while she was crying and still holding her tight.

Jane stated, "I am going to stay with our cousin, Ken, in Tennessee until I get on my feet. I will call Ken when we are on the road but I have to go now."

Karen and Jane stood there crying and holding each other. They were not only family but also best friends because they grew up together in Alabama as children.

Karen also had two children and her little girl Rose was best friends with Jane's daughter Tasha as well. They were both ten years old. They could not believe what was happening. Tasha and Rose held each other, crying in fear they would never see each other again. Allen was angered by this current situation, although the abuse in Jane's household was well known. Allen always stayed out of their family affairs, even though he disagreed with the violence. This was the last straw for Allen who disappeared into the back room as Jane was talking to Karen. Eventually Karen noticed Allen was gone and called out for him. Allen reappeared and walked up to Jane and reached into his pocket and pulled out some money. Allen looked at Karen as she smiled in agreement and he gave Jane 200 dollars.

Allen told Jane, "This isn't much, but it should get you to Tennessee." Then he gave her a hug and told her to be careful and that they would handle things in Alabama.

Karen and her two children left on the 3 A.M. bus to Tennessee. When Jane left Alabama with the children, she never looked back and the cousins never saw each other again.

CHAPTER 3

When you can't remember what happened the night before.

The next day, Marcus woke up to an unfamiliar quietness around the house. He started looking around for his wife and children. He yelled out for Jane, but no one answered. He called for his children and still no one answered. Marcus had a strange feeling in his stomach. Knowing how mean and nasty he was to his wife, he decided to look in the closet to see if she had finally decided to leave him. He looked in both closets and confirmed all their clothes were still in the house. When he saw nothing out of place, he did not suspect anything was wrong. He felt hungry and went to the kitchen for breakfast. Marcus became very angry at his wife once again. He noticed there was no breakfast on the stove for him to eat.

He yelled out, "Lazy old woman couldn't even fix me breakfast before leaving the house." Marcus fixed himself breakfast, then went on with his day doing chores on the land.

As the day went by, Marcus noticed his family had not returned home. It was getting dark and he started getting worried, so he went over to Karen's house to see if Jane was over there. He knocked on the door and Karen's husband, Allen, was already expecting him.

Allen said, "Hello, how are things going?" Allen never revealed his knowledge of what happened the night before.

Jane's husband, Marcus, asked if Allen had seen his wife and children today.

Karen's husband proudly stated, "No, I have not seen your family today." He did not tell a lie because the last time he spoke to them was before midnight.

Marcus seemed angry with Allen's response. They both stared at each other for a moment. Even though Marcus did not believe Allen, he left and he never saw his family again.

CHAPTER 4

*Sometimes the tables do turn
which may not be in your favor.*

As the days grew long, Marcus took up with another woman. One night, he arrived back home drunk and started beating her the same way he had attacked Jane. This woman had meanness inside of her and decided she was not going to be a beaten pole for him. She sat on the couch all bruised up and bleeding. She wanted out of the relationship just as fast as she could. The problem was she wanted to hurt him and thought quickly on how she would do it.

She waited until he was asleep and set the house on fire and blamed it on the open flame in the fireplace. Everyone wanted to know why she did not try to save Marcus from the fire. She stated that he was so drunk and that she could not move him. Everybody believed the story since they knew what type of man Marcus was when he drank.

Jane heard about the tragedy from the grapevine and was so relieved because now she would not have to worry about him ever again. She never looked back and wanted to forget any bad memories she had from her home town. She always prayed for her family and her cousin, Karen, every night before she went to bed. Jane raised her two children with little or no money, but she was at peace.

CHAPTER 5

Can't run away from everything?

As the years passed, Jane's two children Tasha and Anthony grew up in Tennessee and Jane never remarried. Jane was overprotective of her children and did not want them to go through or see abuse ever again. Jane never spoke of their father again and the children never asked. Both children were happy to be out of the abusive household. Jane started working at the local mall. She sent postcards to Karen from time to time, but fell on hard times so the postcards stopped.

Jane's two children grew up close to one another and supported each another. As the years passed, Jane discovered she had breast cancer. The children were devastated. At this time Tasha was married with a teenage daughter. Anthony never married and never had children. Anthony took his mother's illness hard and started going down the road as his father Marcus. Anthony became a nasty drunk and started fights with Tasha daily. He argued about his mother's care and started abusing his female friends.

Jane's illness did not stop her from seeing the road her son Anthony was going down. Jane tried to tell her daughter Tasha not to be mad at him and just pray for him. After her son went on an abusive rage one night with his girlfriend, he was finally put in jail for domestic violence. Tasha went down to the jail and pleaded with Anthony to stop drinking so much. She reminded him again how their father Marcus abused their mother.

Tasha asked him as he was crying in the jail cell and all he could say was, "Please help me sis."

Tasha replied, "Do you want to end up like our father?" Little did Jane know, the children found out their father was burned up in a fire. Tasha continued, "Evil things happen to evil people."

Anthony cried in the jail cell and he shouted, "NO! NO! I promise I will go get help if the Lord gets me out of this. I will sign myself into a clinic and get help."

They both sat there crying at the jail. Tasha's brother received probation because this was his first arrest.

CHAPTER 6

Rehab can be a struggle.

When Anthony was released from jail on probation, he immediately checked himself in a rehabilitation clinic. The first few days were hard for Anthony to handle. Tasha was feeling torn apart as she was split between her mother's bedside and visiting her brother in rehab. Tasha's husband, Andre, and daughter, Cindy, were taking care of the home front, cooking and cleaning at the house. Anthony fought hard daily to overcome drinking. Anthony would write his mother letters and Tasha would read them to her as they arrived.

Anthony started a goal list of things he wanted to do when he left the clinic. The first thing was a promise to his mother to finish his degree. The second thing was to never turn to drinking as a way to get over problems. As Anthony kept the list, he stayed focused on his goals in life. He realized his choices had kept him from getting as far in his life as he could have.

While he was in rehab, his mother took a turn for the worse. Anthony stayed in rehab for six months and was released from rehab two weeks before his mother passed away. Jane had lasted two years after being diagnosed with breast cancer. Tasha was so afraid Anthony would turn back to drinking. Anthony did go into a depressed state, but he channeled that negative energy to finish his degree like he had promised his mother. Anthony only had a few classes to take to complete his degree. He only needed to take one semester of classes. Although it was hard work with long nights trying to avoid the temptation of drinking to ease the stress, Tasha was right there to support her brother.

Tasha was going through her own way of dealing with her mother's death, but she did have her husband and daughter to lean on. She often thought about her cousin Rose from back home when they left in the middle of the night. That traumatic experience haunted Tasha at night sometimes. Tasha always prayed that one day they would see each other again.

Anthony finished his degree in business, became a consultant, and moved to Kentucky. He started dating and never drank again, not even socially. He made a promise on his mother's grave that he would never turn out like his father.

CHAPTER 7

Secrets

At this time, Tasha's daughter, Cindy, was starting college and received a track and field scholarship to a local university. Cindy was very excited to start college and to begin a new outlook on life, but first she had one last event to commemorate her high school journey—prom night! This was her senior prom and the last time she would hang out with her classmates. As the night progressed, one of the seniors revealed he had brought some alcohol to the party. Cindy had never touched alcohol before and did not see any harm in trying it, although she remembered how her uncle had a problem with it.

Cindy thought, "It is only one sip and I can stop whenever I want to."

After Cindy and her friends finished off a bottle of gin, she developed a taste for the alcohol and did not feel it would hurt her in any way. Of course, Cindy did not share this information with Tasha when she returned home after prom. She went straight to bed and made sure her mother and father did not smell anything. Since prom was after graduation and Cindy started college in the summer session, she left for college one week after prom.

As the fall session began, all the students arrived with bubbly eyes, ready for new experiences. Cindy walked onto the field for practice and ran into Erica. Now, Erica was the track and field team's snob and always got her way one way or another. She had the team eating out of her hands. Erica was a sophomore on the team and a very good athlete as well. Siblings Tiny and Charles also arrived for practice. When Erica saw Charles, she knew that was who she wanted.

As practice continued daily, it seemed as if Tiny and Cindy were always competing against one another. Cindy was very humbled and Tiny was very competitive. The first indoor home track meet was coming up and Tiny trained hard to be the best.

CHAPTER 8

Track meet

For the first home track meet of the indoor season, all the parents came out to see their children compete. The track meet was in full swing and all the athletes were primed and ready.

Erica screamed, "OMG! Is Tiny racing against Cindy again in the 60-meter dash?"

"Yep!" shouted the team.

Erica proceeded on, "Why does this girl like to get beat? She should stick to the pole vault or something!"

Tiny always came in second to Cindy.

One of Erica's best friends Lisa asks, "Is that Charles standing against the fence over there? He is so fine."

Erica said, "I can't believe he is even related to Tiny."

Lisa replied, "Right, her brother or maybe he's adopted." They all laughed.

"On your marks, get set, Go!" shouted the official, the gun went off and the race began...

Tiny got a lead off and Cindy coasted in second. Once they reached 30-meters, Cindy just walked Tiny down and won the race without losing her breath. Tiny came in a close second.

Cindy shook Tiny's hand and said, "Keep training. It will be your race one of these days." They both looked at each other and smiled and walked away.

Tiny's mother, Rose, arrived to the meet and sat next to Cindy's mother, Tasha. As the crowd cheered on the race, the two women sitting next to each other struck up a conversation. They both started shouting—one for Tiny and the other for Cindy. Although both girls were teammates and on the same track team, they were very competitive against one another.

CHAPTER 9

The reunion

Rose and Tasha were not competitive type people; they just enjoyed the sport. (Although, they did not know it at the time because it was both girls' freshman year.)

Rose said, "Hello, I am from Alabama. I just landed and had to rush to the meet and could not even check into my hotel yet. I was afraid I would miss something," as she laughed.

Tasha replied, "I understand completely! But you say you are from Alabama? I was born in Alabama, but my mother left when I was very young. I live here in Tennessee and my name is Tasha."

Rose laughed, "I had a favorite cousin named Tasha when I was growing up! We were best friends, but she moved away when I was younger."

Rose remembered a time they went to the creek and Tasha got hurt and badly scarred her knee. Just as she was speaking they looked at each other and starting crying.

Tasha was wearing shorts and pointed to her knee where there was the scar. Tasha looked at Rose and Rose looked at Tasha.

At this point, they both asked at the same time, "What is your mother's name?" At that moment, they started laughing.

Rose asked, What is your mother's name?"

Tasha answered, "Jane." Tasha asked as she pleaded, "Tell me your mother's name is Karen?!"

Rose proclaimed, "Yes it is! Your family left Alabama in the middle of the night and we never saw you again. I missed you so much."

They talked throughout the entire track meet, remembering the last day they saw each other.

Tasha mentioned, "I will never forget that awful night and I was so glad my mother did not stay with my father. That is a bad thing to say but he was a mean old man and she deserved better. I was so proud of her when she just walked away with nothing and started all over. She is my inspiration whenever anything is going haywire. I always tell myself I can handle this, get it together Tasha. I always wonder what really ever happened to good old dad. We heard stories of his death but not the whole truth. We dare not ask mother."

Rose told her he was killed in a house fire not too long after they left. Tasha felt sad for a moment and prayed for his sins and thanked God for protecting her family from him.

Rose asked, "How is your mother and what ever happened to your brother? How is he doing?"

Tasha told her in a sad voice, "My mother died three years ago from breast cancer. My brother took Mom's illness very hard. He started drinking heavily and became abusive like our good ol' dad. It took him getting thrown in jail to realize how abusive he had become."

Rose was so sad for Tasha's family and just gave her a hug.

"My brother is doing awesome now. He finished his degree and has not had a drink since he left rehab. He lives in Kentucky as a consultant."

Rose added, "My mom always talked about your family and wished you well. She said she received postcards from time to time and lost contact when I was in middle school."

The cousins shared family photos and since the track meet was at their children's college, Kingbar University in Tennessee, Tasha insisted Rose stay with her family and not at the hotel. Tasha lived only thirty minutes away from the university.

Rose was so excited and immediately said, "Yes, because I am not letting you out of my sight again!" While the reunited cousins were happy, their children might have a different feeling on the surprise family reunion.

CHAPTER 10

Competition

The track meet was in full competition mode. Tiny and Cindy noticed their mothers were talking to each other in a very friendly manner. Both girls were curious as to what could they be talking about so intently.

Tiny went over to Charles and asked if he knew who their mother was talking to.

Charles looked and said, "No, but Mom sure looks happy with whatever they are talking about."

Cindy overheard the conversation from Tiny and Charles and looked puzzled as well.

Charles started his event in the hurdles and finished third in the race. He raced against his biggest competition in this event since he started racing at fifteen years old. His name was Justin, who attended another college. Justin was listed as "Olympic material" in the hurdles. This was something Charles wanted to be considered for a long time. Charles was always the hardest on himself when it came to his events.

Charles's coach approached him after the event, and stated, "Charles, what happened? You always win that race did you hurt yourself?"

Charles responded, "I don't know what happened. I just felt someone pass me by and I froze in my mind. I could not believe I was getting passed, especially in this event."

Coach mentioned to Charles, "You have to complete your race regardless of what is happening around you. You should know this already, Charles."

Charles looked in the sky with agreement. Tiny waited for Charles to finish talking to his coach as she was warming up for her last race.

Tiny asked, "Charles you good?"

He said "Yeah! I need to stop second guessing myself when I am racing. I know I can beat that guy."

Tiny said, "I know what you mean, but the year just started, and we have plenty more races to get the job done."

"You're right sis!!" Charles smiled.

Tiny started her triple jump competition and ended up placing second in the event. She was happy about this placement since she had not really put her all in the jumps events as much as the racing events. Her coach did tell her she could give a better effort next time she competed. Tiny agreed with her coach and declared that she would train harder on her jumps. Tiny realized if she really focused she might have been placed first in the event.

"Next time coach!" Tiny shouted and the coach walked away.

CHAPTER 11

Curiosity

Cindy walked over to the stands to meet with her mother after the meet. Cindy's mother was laughing with Tiny's mother. Cindy tapped her mother on the shoulder and asked who her new friend was. With a smile, Tasha was so excited to introduce Rose that she was tongue tied.

Tasha finally caught her breath and said, "This my old and dearest friend and cousin from my home town in Alabama. We have not seen each other for thirty years and she is a sight for sore eyes."

Cindy said, "Hello, Ms. Rose, it is very nice to meet you. You must be somebody special because my mom has been smiling the whole time ya'll have been talking during the track meet. Do you have any children on any of the track teams?"

Tasha mentioned, "Yes, actually they both compete on your track team together. They are brother and sister and here they come right now."

Cindy turned around and looked at who was coming over to the stands. It was Tiny and Charles. Cindy mouth dropped open in utter surprise. Rose reached out to hug her children and introduce them to Tasha.

Rose said, "Tiny and Charles, this is my dear old friend and our cousin Tasha."

Tiny and Charles looked and said, "Hello Ms. Tasha!"

Tasha turned around and said, "Hello and this is my daughter, your cousin Cindy."

Tiny and Charles looked at each other and then back at Cindy with their mouths wide open and they all just smiled in front of their mom to hide what they were really thinking. Rose was so excited when she mentioned she would be staying at Tasha's house for the weekend and that she had invited everyone to dinner tonight.

Tiny and Charles could not refuse and replied, "We would be delighted to join you!" While the children were being hugged by their moms, they were confused. They wondered how they could be related, from what family tree, or did the wind blow the leaves from far away to our direction?

"OMG!" thought Cindy. "Do I start hanging out with someone I barely know just because we are family now?"

Charles had no thoughts about the situation; after the initial shock he was okay. He was happy to have a family member close to him, so as to get a home cooked meal once in a while since his mother lived so far away.

Tiny was confused as well and did not know how to proceed from this point. They were not enemies or friends, but teammates on the track team. Only time would tell on how Tiny, Cindy and Charles would open up to the coach on their newfound family tree.

CHAPTER 12

Building Friendship

Erica and Lisa came into the locker room for track practice and noticed Cindy saying hello to Tiny after she came through the door.

Erica turned to Lisa and asked, "What is up with that?"

Lisa replied, "What?"

Erica stated, "Why did Cindy say hi to Tiny? Are they BFFs now or something? Cindy never says hi to anyone when she arrives—not until she goes through her daily routine."

Lisa replied, "Right! Straight to her locker with her headset on blasting, neatly takes out her workout clothes, goes to the restroom, changes, brushes her teeth, and then she's ready to talk to people."

The rest of the team laughed softly since they all knew Cindy was sort of a private person.

Erica continued, "So why is she talking to Tiny now? Not that I am concerned about it at all but what gives?"

Lisa started walking into the weight room area and saw Tiny sitting on the bench. She noticed Cindy walking over to her and pretended like she was working out to try to listen to the conversation.

Cindy walked over to Tiny and said, "Well, I guess we are related and that makes us cousins, right?"

Lisa could not hold her tongue at first and had to grab her mouth so she would not make a sound.

Tiny replied, "Yep, I believe that makes us third cousins within the family tree to be exact!" as she smiled.

Cindy asked Tiny about her workout methods on her sprints. She told her what would help her get out of the blocks sooner and gave her tips on her balance in running. Tiny was surprised with the conversation and very appreciative of the help. Cindy also added when they finished the conversation, "Just to let you know, I help everybody if I see something they can improve on, so I don't want you to think it is because we are family I told you those things. I was going to help you anyway but now we are family maybe we can be more than just teammates. I never had a sister."

Tiny replied, "I would like that because I don't have one either unless you count Charles. He gets on my nerves from time to time."

They both laughed, and Cindy walked out of the weight room. Tiny was happy, but Cindy quickly left because she had a secret she did not want anyone to know just yet.

CHAPTER 13

Secrets

Lisa could not wait to find Erica to give her the juicy news regarding the newly found cousin. Erica was working on her blocks when Lisa came running up to her in a panic.

Lisa shouted, "Erica OMG! You will not believe what I just overheard in the weight room."

Erica, out of breath from working out, could hardly speak. She signaled to Lisa to calm down and talk slowly. Erica was finally able to breathe normally and said, "What… What is it, tell me."

Lisa whispered in Erica's ear what she just overheard and Erica shouted, "I knew something had to have happened! I wonder why they have not shared this information with the team. Are they embarrassed of one another or something? Who cares if they are cousins or not." Erica added, "This changes nothing. I am the captain of the team this year and if anything out of the ordinary goes on, I will be there to catch it."

Lisa nodded her head in agreement.

Erica looked up and noticed Charles working out on the field. *This might be a good thing now. Cindy is off the list for Charles and I can move in for his affection.* "Perfect, watch this."

Erica walked over in the area where Charles was training and just happened to trip on something on the ground. Charles noticed her and reached out to catch her.

Erica said softly, "Oh wow, thank you Charles. I don't know what I tripped over. I am so sorry to interrupt your workout."

Lisa was smiling from ear to ear.

Charles, being the gentleman he is stated, "No problem, are you okay? Be careful and watch where you're walking. You know there could be lumps in the ground from all the sprint spikes we wear while working out on these fields."

Erica replied, "Sure, I will. See you later Charles."

Lisa met her on the side of the track and was very excited by what she saw, but confused because she also had a little crush on him but not as big as the one Erica had. Lisa stayed quiet regarding her feelings and encouraged Erica to pursue Charles.

CHAPTER 14

Happiness

Rose returned home to tell her husband, John, the good news of meeting her cousin, Tasha, whom she spoke of dearly missing since before they were married. John already felt awful from missing the children's track meet; then he missed one of the most important moments in his wife's life! Rose told John that Tasha had one lovely daughter and she lived in the same city as the University. Rose also mentioned she would be able to see more home track meets now since Tasha lived there. Now, she would not have to worry about the hotel cost each time. Rose also told John that they had stayed up late talking and Tasha even called off work the next day so they could do a spa day together. Rose said it was like they were teenagers going to the mall together. She said, "I felt like I got my best friend back again."

John was asking all kinds of questions. Although they still stayed in their home town, he had moved there many years after Tasha's family had left. John and Rose talked about the reunion with her cousin all day.

John was excited for his wife and suddenly he said to Rose, "How was the track meet?"

Rose looked at John and they both started laughing and she apologized for forgetting to tell him about the track meet.

Rose said, "Honey, Tasha and I were talking so much in the bleachers at the track meet I sort of missed a lot of it. I did see Tiny and Cindy compete in the 60-meter dash. Tiny is looking stronger; she finished second. Charles competed in the 60-meter hurdles and finished third overall."

John said "Third? They are hard competitors. WOW! I wish I could have gone to the track meet, but I will not miss the next one." John was the competitor in the family and always pushed the children to the limit and encouraged them to the upmost.

Rose told John, "Yeah, they might have needed you there because you know I am worthless when it comes to being competitive."

John agreed, "Right, but I am so happy you found your cousins and at a track meet no doubt. God works out his miracles in his own way. Rose, for what you have told me, from what you remember, she lived a difficult life in the beginning. It seems she has overcome her obstacles in her past and grew up to be a strong woman like you are, Rose. I really hope and pray you never lose contact with your cousin Tasha again."

CHAPTER 15

Reminiscing

Rose told John that Tasha had a daughter who competed against Tiny in the sprints and she always seemed to beat her too.

John had to admit, "If I did know they were kin, I would say something about that, but it is in the blood. Rose, you remember telling me the one time when you were five, you and Tasha raced up to the creek. You said before you thought about starting to run Tasha was five feet in front of you. The apple doesn't fall to far from the tree, right!"

Rose started laughing as she also remembered that rare moment in her past. "You are so right, but Tiny is so much faster than I was and she did not even run her time in the race, so I know she can do better."

As the two were talking, the phone rang and John answered. John said, "Hello, what can I do for you today?" It was his daughter Tiny on the other line.

Tiny said "Hey, Dad, how are you doing? I really missed you at the track meet. Are you coming to the next one? I know you heard about Mom meeting her cousin here at the meet the other day. What do you think about that? Now I have a cousin in my track team! She seems cool, but I don't know? Dad, are you listening to me? Why have you not said anything?"

John, knowing when his daughter called she would ask several different questions before anyone could get a word in, finally said, "Hello, and I missed you too. Yes, yes, I think it is amazing for her to reconnect with her family and she is so happy. You know when Tasha is happy, I am happy. I think it will take time to get to know anybody you just meet, but she is family, so no matter what, you will have to learn how to get along. She is going to be a frequent flyer family member and not an in and out family member, if you know what I mean." They both laughed and agreed.

Tiny mentioned, "I am so happy Mom has found her best friend and cousin from her childhood! Since Charles and I are out of the house, I know Mom felt lonely and now she's reunited with Ms. Tasha—this could not have happened at a more perfect time. God's surprises and miracles are at work daily!"

"Hey," her dad mentioned, "that's what I was saying. I wonder where you got your thinking from?" Both of them started laughing. "Where is Charles, is he close to you, Tiny?"

"No, he is on the track working out. He told me to let you know he loves you and he missed you also at the meet. He will call you later tonight."

"Tiny I heard from your mother you and Charles were not at your best at the past track meet. What in the world was going on with you guys? Do I need to talk to the coach or do I need to come up on the regular to make sure practice is really taking place?"

Tiny replied, "No Dad, all is good. We are just getting our minds focused on the team workout program together. This is college now and we are getting our feet wet. We will be fine. Please do not worry yet, Dad. You know how anxious you get with competition."

"I know sweetie. I promised your mom I would stay low for the first few months, so that is all the time you have until I get on the scene and become Big Old Overbearing Dad."

Tiny replied, "I will let Charles know and thank Mother. Dad, I have to go now. I love you, send my love to Mom."

John shouted, "Tiny says she loves you and goodbye."

Rose shouted, "Goodbye sweetie. Love you both!" as she was singing and feeling happy.

John said, "Goodbye honey," hung up the phone, glanced at his wife and smiled.

CHAPTER 16

Repeating History

Tiny hung up the phone with a puzzled look on her face and went to the locker room to change clothes. Just as she opened her locker, there was a bottle sticking out from the back of it. Tiny was shocked. It was the pills she had started taking since she was in college and she did not want anyone to know she was taking them.

The coach walked up behind her and started talking. She slammed the locker shut with surprise and shouted, "Wow, you surprised me coach… um what's up?"

Coach told her she was doing well but she noticed a change in her attitude and on the track. She wanted to know if there was anything wrong that she wanted to talk about.

Tiny answered, "No ma'am, all is okay with me."

The coach told her, "You know my door is always open. I am not just the coach, I am a friend and I support and care about each and every person on this campus."

Tiny look puzzled and answered, "Okay, and I appreciate that coach and will keep that in mind."

Coach walked away and Tiny was relieved the coach did not see anything. Tiny was a little bit worried about what the coach had just told her about her attitude change. Tiny had not noticed she had changed in attitude but that was something she would have to take into account from now on.

The last thing Tiny wanted was for anyone to find out she was taking pills for anything. Tiny parents were strict and she didn't want to add to the conversation on the new pills she started taking after she left for college. She was afraid her parents would not understand why she was taking these pills. She tried to talk to Charles regarding the pills but was afraid he might tell their parents because he could get overprotective at times. Tiny got dressed and left the locker room. She ran into Charles and they walked to the dorms together.

CHAPTER 17

Roommates

Since this college offered coed dorms, the brother and sister had to room together. This was Tiny and Charles' first year in college away from home. Of course, they did not want to room together, but to avoid arguments and disappointing their parents they agreed to room together for the first year only. Their parents agreed with only the first year as roommates which made them feel much safer so their kids could could watch after each other.

The coed dorm room was awesome. It was a two bedroom condo with a private bathroom in each room. The room came with a common area which included a full kitchen, washer, dryer, and living room. Once the siblings researched the room arrangements, they agreed that since they could still shut their door and be alone when they wanted to have privacy like being at home, the first year wouldn't be that bad.

Tiny had no problem keeping her secret from her brother since each room had its own personal lock on the door. As Tiny and Charles were walking home, Tiny tried to bring up her secret but Charles interrupted her with questions about Cindy and Tasha. Charles could not stop talking about the home cooking he was going to eat every weekend.

Tiny just laughed and said, "You know we do have a kitchen in our apartment. You can cook your own home cooked meal. Mom taught both of us how to cook three course meals. That is one of the reasons Mom liked the kitchen in our room and purchased all that food in our refrigerator." Tiny mentioned, "Remember that Charles?" as she laughed. "OHHH I know what it is. You are expecting me to cook for you every day aren't you?"

Charles looked at Tiny and started smiling.

"OHHHH no buddy, you can cook for yourself and maybe, just maybe, I will cook something for you, maybe bro." They both just laughed and Tiny never got around to her secret.

CHAPTER 18

Hanging out

It was late and Tiny was hanging out with Cindy. She decided to confide in Cindy and tell her the secret. Cindy noticed Tiny was very nervous when they were together and asked what the problem was. Just as Cindy was asking about Tiny, Tiny noticed a bottle of alcohol sticking out of Cindy's jacket. Tiny did not say anything right then.

Tiny stated, "I have something to tell you and I am very nervous about it. My family has no idea about this secret."

Cindy was worried it was something awful and told Tiny, "No matter what it is I will help you any way I can."

Concerned, Tiny paused and looked toward Cindy's pocket again, then before she brought up her issue regarding the pills, she paused again. Tiny asked Cindy, "Is that a bottle of alcohol sticking out of your jacket pocket?"

Cindy looked surprised that Tiny had seen the bottle. Cindy replied quickly, "Yeah, I was just trying it a little," knowing she had already started drinking but not wanting to answer any more embarrassing questions.

They were both in sports and the university had no tolerance for drugs or alcohol.

Tiny replied, "Please don't take this the wrong way but your uncle and grandfather both had a drinking problem, right?"

Cindy replied ashamed, "Yeah why? Just because they had a drinking problem does not mean I will. Besides, I have not tried it yet." This was a lie. "I just wanted to see what the big deal was all about."

Tiny looked puzzled for a moment and smiled and started to speak. "I know we just met Cindy, but you don't have a drinking problem, do you? I know you said you have never touched the stuff, but you seem too nervous about it."

Cindy replied, "NO! I am not like my uncle. All I wanted to do is taste it that is all. I can throw it away whenever I want to."

Tiny asked, "Well that bottle does not look full, so where did you get it?"

Cindy shook her arms when she noticed Erica in the area. This created enough distraction to end the conversation, which was a huge relief for Cindy.

CHAPTER 19

Misunderstanding

At the moment Erica and Lisa walked by, Tiny stopped talking.

Erica walked over and said, "Well, if it isn't the new family tree hanging out like leaves." Erica and Lisa laughed together.

Tiny got up and left the table and Cindy followed her, giving Erica and Lisa an angry look.

Cindy caught up with Tiny, "Stop, Tiny and tell me what is going on."

Tiny looked at Cindy and said, "I started taking birth control pills when I came to college."

Cindy replied in shock, "Birth control pills! Why are you taking birth control pills and why are you afraid to tell your family? Does your father know you are taking them?"

Tiny stated, "NO! No one knows about it because my family feels if you're taking the pill you must want to start having sex but that is not the case yet. I don't want to get into a relationship and be too late to start taking the pill."

Cindy asked, "Are you dating someone Tiny?"

Tiny said, "Yes, we started seeing each other before I left for college and I really like him. I thought it would be a responsible thing to do to start birth control pills just in case things get heated." Tiny started blushing.

Cindy asked, "Does he go to the college here with you. Who is he?"

Tiny stated, "No, he goes to another college not far from here and he runs track also and we have some track meets together. He competes against Charles a lot. Actually, he beat Charles in the 60-meter hurdle race in the last meet. "

Cindy could hardly believe who she was talking about. "OMG! Scott! He is a catch, really cute and a head on his shoulders. I see why you are a little afraid to tell Charles, but you need to tell your parents you are taking those pills."

Tiny stated, "I know, I know but how? My mom will freak out thinking I'm planning on having sex, which I am not, but I just have to be covered. You know what I mean, Cindy?"

Cindy said, "I know you need to tell your mom as soon as possible and not later. She will understand, trust me. She was young once and although she will flip, she will land on her feet and listen to you. It is all part of growing up and becoming a responsible adult. She will be angry, but she will have to respect your decision. You are of age and she cannot stop you from taking the pills. She *will* want to meet your new boy toy. Ha ha! Sorry to laugh, but get ready for all the questions. Be prepared is all I am saying."

Tiny agreed, "You are right I will be ready."

"Well, I got to go, Tiny. See you in the morning. It is getting late."

Tiny looked at Cindy. "Now we both know what you have to do as well. You need to tell your mother you are having these urges for drinking alcohol."

Cindy seemed annoyed at Tiny.

Tiny grabbed her arm. "Cindy I just found a cousin/sister and I don't want to lose you for a stupid mistake. I have something to lose and you do too." Tiny and Cindy said their goodbyes.

Tiny was tired and arrived home late. She took her pill in the kitchen since she took her birth control at night. She opened the container to take her medication, forgot to throw it away from tiredness, and left the package on the counter.

The next morning Charles was in the kitchen making breakfast and noticed a package on the counter. Being the big brother and a nosy person, he read the package. Since it was early, and he was half asleep, he had to reread the package twice to see it really said birth control pills, with Tiny's name on it. He could hardly believe what he was reading and became wide awake at that point.

Tiny woke up early every morning and walked into the kitchen. Charles looked at her and handed her the package with a smirk on his face.

She looked at him and begged him not to tell Mom or Dad yet. "I am going to tell them, OK?!"

Charles asked, "I just want to know who you are doing this for? Do I need to have a talk with somebody? And I hate to ask this—do I know this boy?"

Tiny could not speak for a minute. She caught her breath and said, "Hmmm, well no, I am not doing this for anyone and NO, I am not having sex yet. The boy? You know his name, Scott, and he goes to another school. He competes against you in track."

Charles looked puzzled and said, "SCOTT! The one I ran against on the meet Scott?"

Tiny said "Yes..."

"Well, at least you picked a sporty guy and I don't really know him, so I guess... Well, know you can give me the inside track and tell me when he is sick or something LOL right?"

Tiny just looked at him and smirked.

Charles said, "Well, it is one thing you have to do now and that is to tell our parents the good news. I don't know why you feel you need to start taking pills, but I will support you in this if you want me to Tiny."

Tiny looked at Charles and said "Thank you! I really appreciate you supporting me. "

CHAPTER 20

Truths

Three weeks had passed and Tiny still had not told her parents about the birth control pills. Tiny was visiting home one weekend and her mother noticed a pharmacy bag on the bathroom counter in Tiny's room. Of course, Rose was curious about the package and opened it. When Rose read what it said and the name on the package she could not believe her daughter was having sex. Rose called her husband at work immediately and told him what she found. He told Rose to calm down and that they would handle it together tonight. He asked where Tiny was at and Rose stated she was at the mall with her friends.

"We will talk to her tonight Rose, so don't mention this issue to her until we are together."

"Okay, honey."

"I know you're upset. Give Tiny a chance to explain herself before we bulldozer her with questions.

Remember honey, Tiny is of age to have the pills and take them without our permission."

Rose stated, "Are you inhaling fumes or something? I don't care how old she is or how old she thinks she is. She should have at least told me what was going on. I am her mother! I thought we had such a close relationship. I feel like I am losing my little girl."

"Honey, she is a grown woman making her own choices and mistakes. Trust me, we will get to the bottom of this tonight. Relax, but I have to go... Talk to you tonight."

Rose replied, "Okay, I will try and you know this will be hard for me but I will do it... WHEW. Why me, Lord?"

Tiny arrived back home and said hello to her mother. Rose looked puzzled as if she did not know how to respond.

She finally said, "Hey sweetie, how was the mall?"

Tiny started talking about all the fun the girls had at the mall. At this point, Rose was listening, but not listening and day dreaming about her little girl growing up. All of a sudden Rose heard Tiny calling out for her.

Tiny called, "Mom, mom, mom... are you listening to me, Mom?"

Rose shook her head and said, "I am sorry honey, what were you saying again? I must have been day dreaming for a second. Sorry honey, so.... how was the mall again?"

Tiny asked her mom if she was okay because she was acting strange.

Rose replied, "I am fine."

Tiny started talking about the mall all over again.

A few hours went by and John came home. Rose could hardly wait to get her husband alone in a room. She was bursting and the seams on her face could hardly contain her feelings. "Tiny is in her room, so how do you want to handle this?"

Rose's husband looked at her and said, "This is not mission impossible, we are just going to come straight out and ask her about it."

Rose replied "Good plan good plan... break..."

He said, "Break? What is that?"

She stated, "Don't you say that when you come out of a huddle and going into game plan mode?"

He looked at his wife and shook his head. "Honey relax, let's take this slow. Okay, babe?"

Rose called Tiny to the front room. Tiny came down, saw her dad and gave him a big hug.

He told Tiny, "There's something your mother and I want to talk to you about."

Tiny had no clue what they wanted and sat down waiting with excitement.

Rose started the conversation and said, "First of all, I was not eavesdropping or snooping, not much that is... anyway, I found that bag with your birth control pills in them."

Tiny eyes lit up and she was horrified and did not know what to do next.

At this point, her father said, "Honey we are here for you. All we want is an explanation on why you decided to start taking these pills and when. We have always been an honest family and able to talk about everything. Your mother and I really want to know why you feel you had to hide this from us?"

Tiny was surprised and afraid to say anything. In her mind, she was thinking, *Is this a trick of no screaming and yelling, or pulling out the Bible... Hmmm is this a trap? Lord help me, let me know what to do next, I will not lie to my parents so the truth it is… Here we go.*

"Well, Mom and Dad, I started taking the pills shortly after I left for college. I went to a local parent planning clinic and got the prescription. Just to let you both know, no, I am not having sex yet. I am still a virgin. I did start seeing this guy a few months ago."

Of course, her parents' eyes lit up and they looked at each other but kept quiet until the end—although, they wanted to scream and shout. Tiny told them everything about the boy, when and where they met. She even informed them they are not even talking about sex, but it was something she wanted to do. Tiny told them the boy did not even know she was taking birth control pills. After a long conversation about everything, Tiny's parents were proud of their daughter in many ways. They commended her on how responsible she was and asked her if she ever decided to cross over to the other side with sex, to please not tell them for a long, long, long time.

Tiny said "Deal!"

When Tiny arrived back at the dorms, she found her bother and Cindy walking back from track. "Hey guys, What's up?" Tiny asked.

They both replied, "Just working out."

Cindy asked, "How was your trip to home?"

Tiny could not wait to tell them what happened with her parents that weekend. Charles' mouth was wide open, and Cindy was so proud of Tiny for not keeping it a secret anymore. Tiny was relieved to not have to hide anything from her parents.

Erica walked by with her shadow of friends and gave Charles a look like she wanted to eat him up. Cindy and Tiny laughed at Charles. Charles looked at them both and said, "What are you two laughing at?"

Tiny replied, "You lover boy! You know Erica has a huge crush on you and I think you like her too."

Charles said, "So what if I do like Erica?"

Cindy stated, "We don't care about your liking that girl. She is crazy and you can have her. Maybe if you do date her she will stop looking at us crazily."

Tiny and Cindy just laughed and they all split and went their separate ways.

Rose called Tasha to get moral support from the huge news she just encountered from her daughter.

Tasha answered the phone. "Hello? Rose, is that you... Omg! Rose how are you doing today?"

Rose replied, "I am going crazy girl! God works in many ways and I am so glad you are back in my life again."

Tasha asked, "What is wrong Rose?"

"Nothing, just that I found out Tiny is taking birth control pills since her starting college."

Tasha replied, "You did not know or have you two ever talked about it before?"

Rose answered, "No, I always told her focus on her studies and leave that boy stuff until she is older."

Tasha replied, "Well, I guess she is older now and you have to give her room to breathe, Rose. I remembered when I had the huge talk with Cindy about boys. I did not want to explain anything to my little girl, but it was time for her to understand what was coming her way, especially, when she leaves for college. I did not want anyone else telling her anything about the world."

Rose said, "I guess you are right and it does not make me any happier that she is growing up. I am happy she is responsible enough to get the pills. She told us she was not having sex yet, but wanted to be prepared if that moment happens to arrive. Of course, I hope she waits until she is married."

Tasha said, "Right, like we did," and they both laughed and kept enjoying each other's conversation until they lost track of time. Both Tasha and Rose's husbands had arrived home from work when they realized how late it was and needed to get off the phone. It was funny, while they were talking, they both cooked dinner and did laundry. What a way to multitask. They hung up the phone, but before they said good bye they arranged a day Tasha's family would visit Roses' this time.

Tasha's husband asked, "Where is the track meet schedule, so I can try to go to some of the home meets?"

When Rose hung up, her husband asked the same thing. Little did the two ladies know their husbands had been communicating for weeks to get the cousins back together again.

As the year came to an end, the fall indoor track season was off and running. Rose's husband and Tasha's husband started arranging a track meet day for them all to meet. They first asked the ladies which track meet they were attending again together. Once they found that out, they arranged for dinner and flowers at an inclusive restaurant to finally celebrate the union. The husbands were just excited as they found each other because both the ladies talked about each other like they grew up together and never parted. They could feel the love they had for one another. Once all the planning was done, the husbands put their plans into action.

Using the children as bait, the offspring could not wait to help with the surprise. The only other surprise was that Tiny was going bring her new man, Scott, and Charles would be bringing Erica. Only Tiny and Charles's father knew the children were bringing dates, so the siblings had no idea what each other was doing. Their father thought it was time for their mother to meet everyone in a cheerful environment such as this one. Rose's husband almost spoiled the surprise the night before, when Rose asked him what he was doing for the day tomorrow.

Rose's husband half sleep answered, "Meeting with…" and he caught himself just as he was talking and said, "Meeting with some clients. Nothing special."

Rose said, "Okay, make sure you eat a good dinner."

He replied, "Sure will. All of it," and he smiled as he turned over to go to sleep.

CHAPTER 21

New Beginnings

During the track meet, Rose and Tasha were making their own dinner plans for the night. The children kept coming up to the stands one by one, dropping hints about what to do for dinner and where to go. Their moms were puzzled because they did not even invite the children. This was going to be ladies night tonight. Toward the end of the meet, Cindy came up to the stands and insisted they all go out to eat after the meet. Tasha was surprised and looked at Rose.

Rose replied, "Sure, sounds good to me."

Cindy stated, "And I know where to go to, Le'na's Bistro."

Tasha looked with her eyes wide open and replied, "That place requires a reservation. Don't you know it's usually for a special occasion?"

Cindy smiled and mentioned, "Maybe, but let's go by and see if they have room before we have to go to another place. It is just right down the street, right?"

Tasha replied, "Yes it is right down the street. It won't hurt to stop by."

Rose was ready to go, but she had not told her children the plans. Rose stated, "I hope my children don't have plans tonight so they can go."

Cindy replied "They are going! I asked them earlier and they said they are all for it."

After the last track event of the day finished, the moms waited in the stands for the children to change clothes.

In the locker room, Cindy and Tiny were so excited about the surprise for their mothers. Erica walked by getting ready pretty fast from the meet. It was unlike her to move fast after the meet was over. Erica did not say a word or look up at anybody while she was getting dressed.

Tiny told Cindy, "Oh yea, Charles said he will meet us at the restaurant."

Cindy asked, "Is Scott going to be there too?"

Tiny said, "Yes, he is meeting my parents for the first time and I am so nervous, I never brought a boy home to the house ever. OMG! I am freaking out."

Cindy laughed and said, "It will be fine so relax and breathe. Ha ha."

The girls met Tasha and Rose at the bleachers and they started to split to each other's mothers' car.

Tiny mentioned, "Mom, why are we driving in separate cars? That makes no sense."

Tasha agreed and insisted the group ride together to meet Charles. They all piled into Tasha's car and off they went to check out the restaurant. Charles had already arrived at the place and parked as he and his date were waiting in the building for them to walk in. At this point, Charles's father walked up behind him to inform him of the rest of the plans for the evening. Charles's father had already arranged plans with the greeters for what they needed to do when the ladies arrive. Charles told the greeters what his name was so they could let the ladies know he had arrived. The girls would be the point people on informing the greeters which ladies to address after they arrived at Le'na's Bistro.

The ladies finally arrived and found a parking spot. They walked into Le'na's Bistro. Cindy signaled the greeters and they jumped into action. Tasha walked up to the desk and asked if they had any available tables.

The greeters replied, "No, but we have the private room available for you if you would like to be seated in that area. There will only be a few people in the room. Would that be okay with you, madam?"

Tasha replied, "That would be perfect," with a huge smile. She also mentioned they had another person coming that would be joining them.

The greeter answered, "I think your party is already here. Is his name Charles?"

Tiny answered, "Yes, thank you!"

At this time, Tiny was looking out for her date, Scott, to arrive as well. Since it was an overnight meet, he was still in town to join in on the fun. Tasha and Rose followed the greeter to the table and as soon as the doors opened up to the private room, the husbands greeted the ladies with a huge hug and a bouquet of flowers. The children were all smiling and laughing. Tiny and Cindy noticed Erica in the room and Charles hugging her.

The girls looked at each other and said, "About time."

They walked over to Erica, greeted her and rough housed Charles. At this moment, Cindy noticed the liquor in the room and could not keep her eyes off it. Cindy did all she could to avoid the urge to stand close to it but it was calling her to the table. Tasha was enjoying herself but noticed her daughter acting strangely. She looked at her face, then followed her eyes. At this moment, Tiny also was watching Cindy and she saw her mother watching her. Tasha noticed Cindy was staring at the alcohol on the table and that was Tasha's worse fear. She instantly walked over to her daughter, leaned over, and whispered in her ear to accompany her to the restroom. Tiny noticed them leaving the room.

Of course, Cindy agreed, and soon as the door shut to the restroom door, Tasha turned to Cindy.

Tasha quietly said, "I am going to ask you this one time and do not lie to me."

Cindy's mother had never approached her in this way. Cindy started to speak and Tasha interrupted her.

Tasha said in a quiet stern voice, "Cindy, I am your mother and I love you. I know firsthand what alcohol has done to this family. It is hereditary and if you have started drinking or feel like you want to drink, I need to know right now. I repeat, I am here to help you, but you have to help yourself."

Cindy was ashamed to speak but in a soft voice said, "I started drinking at prom night. All the kids were doing it and I just wanted to try it."

Tasha felt she failed as a parent to not see the signs. After the shock of the news became reality, Tasha asked, "How many times have you tried it since prom night?"

Cindy replied, "I started drinking it on weekends on my down time. I don't have a problem, Mom, trust me."

Tasha replied, "That is what they all said, but before you start having a problem we are going to get you help. I told you before I cannot hold your hands, your decision is your own. You know my history with drunken abuse from my father and your uncle. I can't risk losing you."

They started crying and hugging each other and Cindy cried out, "I am so sorry Mom. I am so sorry, I don't want to be like that."

Tasha replied softly, "You will not turn out like that, but we have to work together to fight this now. New Beginnings start today." Tasha told Cindy, "It will not be easy but your father and I will be here for you."

They returned to the celebration and when they entered the room Tiny noticed Cindy had been crying. Cindy and Tiny locked eyes and Cindy smiled and knotted her toward Tiny. This was an indication she just told her mom about the drinking issue. They both smiled at each other.

Once everybody was calming down in the room, Scott walked in.

"Wow, look who just walked in, Tiny. Is he here for you?" Charles said in a deep voice.

Erica could not believe her eyes when she saw Scott walk in the room and to see Tiny no doubt. Tiny greeted Scott and walked him over to her parents. Rose was excited to finally meet her children's dates and they all sat down to have dinner.

"This is a celebration!" John said with happiness. "Let's toast." John could not think of the correct words to say but at the same time everybody at the table shouted out "New Beginnings!!"

ABOUT THE AUTHOR

Living in Detroit, Michigan (Highland Park to Royal Oak Township), I witnessed poverty firsthand because I was a part of it. I had to grow up quickly in my elementary school years and learn survival skills. When I was sixteen I gave birth to my son, then at nineteen married my high school sweetheart after graduation. One thing I did feel throughout my life was LOVE and comfort from my mother. I had a village of family, special shout out to my second mom Aunt Dorothy, to turn to when I was growing up, so although life may have seemed awful by the naked eye, I generally felt happy. My goal is to embrace the love and support I received in my upbringing and be a village for whomever I come in contact with throughout my life.

Now, I'm divorced with three adult children and one daughter-in-law, along with two grandchildren and one on the way. I would like to give Special Thanks to my daughter Lynette as I finish this book. Her assistance with editing and rereading helped me get to the point of publishing. I can't express how I appreciate and love all my children: Bobby Jr., Jonathan and Lynette for the love and support each of them displayed as I embarked on this writing journey.

www.ingramcontent.com/pod-product-compliance
Lightning Source LLC
Chambersburg PA
CBHW071414290426
44108CB00014B/1826